T0129868

# Glimpses through Time

# Glimpses through Time

## Dwight Bernard

# GLIMPSES THROUGH TIME

Copyright © 2019 Dwight Bernard.

All rights reserved. No part of this book may be used or reproduced by any means, graphic, electronic, or mechanical, including photocopying, recording, taping or by any information storage retrieval system without the written permission of the author except in the case of brief quotations embodied in critical articles and reviews.

iUniverse books may be ordered through booksellers or by contacting:

iUniverse
1663 Liberty Drive
Bloomington, IN 47403
www.iuniverse.com
1-800-Authors (1-800-288-4677)

Because of the dynamic nature of the Internet, any web addresses or links contained in this book may have changed since publication and may no longer be valid. The views expressed in this work are solely those of the author and do not necessarily reflect the views of the publisher, and the publisher hereby disclaims any responsibility for them.

Any people depicted in stock imagery provided by Getty Images are models, and such images are being used for illustrative purposes only.
Certain stock imagery © Getty Images.

ISBN: 978-1-5320-6812-6 (sc)
ISBN: 978-1-5320-6813-3 (e)

Print information available on the last page.

iUniverse rev. date:  02/22/2019

# *Introduction*

This book of words and moods, is an expression of the mind and heart. It's a collection of expressions over a period of time. It seeks to reflect views and perceptions, fundamentally fuelling the fire of free expression through word art.

As you read, you will observe various moods and themes, so enjoy, and thanks for reading.

All are expression, word from yours truly,

Dwight A. Bernard
October 2016

# Celestial Bliss

I must be strong, can't afford to be weak,
Hopeless negative, isolating the positive,
Even though the rigors of life surrounds,
me like an angry sea.
Lashing violently against my banks,
My solemn wish is to always be myself.

I must be rational,
Cant be otherwise, its the pathway,
To our conscience, that internal person,
Who controls our false ego
And directs our perceptions and manifestations.
I must be true,
Whats a tragedy to lie,
To attach ones self to such unrealistic,
Stigma, one so narrow, so void.
Without remorse, having no place,
In our chaotic society,
My entire being is over whelmed with celestial gladness.
I sought solace and found in myself,
Found this special thing, i thought didn't exist.

# *Friends*

Friends, together we have trodded
The fantasies of life,
Laughing boyishly,
As we recall our past exploits.
Friends, together we have,
Incline our minds,
As we sought to recreate,
Seeking peace and serenity,
In the arms of our friendship.

No distance can separate,
Our minds, our thoughts.
Together we have explore d the realms,
Of the unknown, searching for,
True happiness and comfort.
Friends, forever we will be,
Friends for all time, until the end.

# Solitude

Where! Oh please show me.
How to rid my mind of all,
The memories of you.
Memories that haunts me
Like a horrid nightmare.
If only i could find a place, where my mind would be at ease.
   Aplace a quiet place, where i can find peace,
   Where! i can't afford to hide myself,
I have to find myself some pleasure,
But i will have to be cautious, taking measures,
Making sure its reality, not a fantasy.
If only i could find a place, someone,
Somewhere, oh, please show me

# *Provocative Nature*

I was born to love nature,
And all that are tied within its wonderful rapture.
Brilliant sunshine, so golden
So radiant so heavenly.
Seems to send its tentacles of gold,
Far beyond the rugged valley
Where the air is freshened by,
The clean perfumely scents of,
Wild roses and blooming jasmines.
Its feeling so heavenly,
As bees buzzed about like angels,
Preparing nectar for mans delight.
Being with nature, gives a mans
Soul tranquility, something so rare,
Nature is everything, so unpredictable, yet heavenly.
So natural in its element, without bliss.

# *I will always remember*

I sat alone, sorrowful, close to tears.
As the tears, the anguish burn deep within.
My only love is gone.
What have i done,
What must i do.
Do i deserve this heartache,
What we had was love,
As pure as water, something you could feel,
From a distance.

Memories so enchanting, yet haunting,
A feeling so strong, without guile, so graceful.
Your face, your smile, your touch,
I know i will not forget,
Will remain a memory, a song,
So refreshing, so new, so profound.

# The Maghreb (sunset)

Darkness fell with a crashing flicker.
Twilight is here it said.
Across the ashen horizon.
Myriad in colors and so swift as the amazon,
A sight so magical, one so majestic.
To sit beside the one you love,
With the maker in control.
Watching as the twilight unfolds,
with pulsating rays, now darkened.
Surely did stir my imagination,
As twilight sings its final tune.
And as the twilight settles with a final light,
Saying goodbye to daylight,
It seems to sends a message to the moon,
To come and provide the next celestial bright.
For me twilight is most welcome,
Awakening my spirit, makes me feel so right.

# *They dream of hate*

They dream only of hate,
This dream, this stigma to which they cling.
Innately hidden in the faucets of their mind,
Blanketed by their ignorance of self,
So they wallow in their self pity and arrogance.
I see the picture they paint,
One we should try to eradicate, evade,
So vivid, one so quaint.
They dream only of hate,
This horror from their childhood.
There is so much hate,
Its make me cold within.
So penetrating, so deep, so deep.
And yet i am joyous completely,
To hate, the thought is beneath me,
I can't live to hate, i hate to hate.

# Whims and fancies

With eyes so boldly shapened,
Eyes colored black, a beauty, She stared at me
This bold eye maiden, sparkling.
With love so over powering,
A soul so laden, yet provocative,
Seeing her for a fleeting moment,
She always seems to fade.
However erratic her actions are,
There is no doubt in my mind
She's my attraction, my distraction.
I reached for her calmly,
And i grasped nothing and i was afraid,
She seems to vanish magically.
Between fantasy and reality,
Is it a dream?
Because she always reemerge,
Leaving me beyond words,
With whims and fancies,
Silent, speechless, tongue tied.

# *From the hill*

He hailed from the hills,
This weary swaggy man
And with himwacs his tool, and a bunch of banana,
Held with great skills.
Patched and torn his clothes, polka dot by sweat and stain
And as his haggard figure loomed across
I knew he was farmer by heart.
Hey!Its time to rest, but he only smiled,
I knew he would never quit.
And whistling, he went his merry way.
Down the road to start a new day.

Truly i am most impressed of this man,
He is a true provider, a son of the soil.
Iwatched him for a while,
He has been my trusted friend, from i was a child.

# Fly away

One day i will fly away
To be free like the birds, free as the trees.
I will soar so high, gliding through the sky.
Leaving all these fantasies behind.
One day i will fly away,
To find peace and solitude,
To find joy, detaching all my emotions,
Free as the breeze, the bees,
Leaving all these ills behind.
One day i will fly away,
And emerse myself in nature's arm.
Embracing all the luxuries of time,
Inclining towards the wishes of nature,
Leaving all these whims behind.
One day i'll fly away
No more will i be a figure or,
A shadow nor a memory,
Etched in the spaces of yesterday,
Forever gone, forever gone,
Leaving this world.

# rReggae

Reggae, the heart throb, the heart beat,
Of our jamaican people, the music of our voices,
The medium of joy, as dancehall fanatics,
Grinds and jigs frantically,
To the magical power of the reggae spirit.
This magic, this gift, this sound,
This pulsating rhythm of reggae,
Brings a merry message of peace and love,
So true and divine.
As the ears gets the pitch,
And the brain tells
the body to move,
To vibrate, as the tempo is felt miles away.
Reggae is African, has perspective,
As the magical congo drums pounds through,
The soul, sending sweet harmony.
Reggae has been our communal voice,
The voice of the anguished, the down trodden,
The destitute, the little yute.

# I stood Alone – A tribute to winnie mandela

I stood alone, i watched helplessly,
As the tyrants went away triumphantly,
With the love of my life,
My strength, my rock, my shield.
And i was alone, so alone,
I stood lonely for twenty-seven years.
On that day, that fateful day,
A part of me went with him too.
He has done all he could,
His captivity was inevitable.
Made possible by a despotic system,
Merciless, inhumane and unjust.
And that day i knew, i had job to do,
To fill a large void, to continue the fight.
I waited, but not alone, he was always there,
And liberty came, through blood, sweat and tears,
Yet i stood firm, i stood tall, refusing to allow myself to fall.

# Last Dance

This is my last dance with you.
So i'm going to give you my all tonight,
For days i've been wanting to let you know,
That I know you're seeing someone else.
This is my last dance with you,
And i wish this wasn't goodbye
I know i gave it my all, my everything,
But now my ship is about to sink,
I guess by now you're happy,
My world has now fallen apart

This is my last dance with you,
Hope you'll find joy and happiness,
I know i have to be strong,
Can't deny, we had it good,
But i guess i was wrong.

This is my last dance with you,
So tonight i'm going to hold you,
Cause we'll never pass this way again
My sadness is overbearing,
But love has this hold on me

This is my last dance with you,
Lady after all we've been through.
There are no regrets, so let's slow dance,
Let's dance the night away.

# My Island Jamaica

Oh my island Jamaica,
My little paradise in the sun,
Where the cool breeze is always blowing,
Island of peenie wallie, beaches, tan and rum.
Scenic beauty and exotic flora
From Kingston to MontegoBay,
There are many places to stay.
Beautiful paradise, the land of sugar cane
Redstripe beer and the good old rum.
From Trelawny to Kingston,
Our athletes are world class.

Jamaica has the fastest man and woman alive,
Jamaica's cess is still the best,
From Negril point to ST. Elizabeth
Our music and icons are without contest
Mountains, rivers, gullies and streams,
Jamaica's water is pure and clean
With diverse class and cultural heritage,
From Cornwall, Middlesex to Surrey county,
Attractions galore, tourists don't have to hurry,
The island of no problem no worry,
We have been on the world stage,
Gorgeous supermodels and superstars,
Jamaica, we little but we talawah.

Tropical heaven, Caribbean gem,
Sweet, sweet jamaica, come and bring a friend
And as we welcome all to our land,
How can we forget the song of the Banana Man
Finger licking jerks, and sweet curried goat,
With manish waterl to wash it down
Oh sweet Jamaica, my Island in the sun.

# It's Amazing

It's amazing, how we view the world as a glimpse,
Through the mirror of time, to find,
Because as human s we struggle,
To find this balance, to be part of something great.

It's amazing how our minds, can be our enemy,
Yet can be our truest friend.
So we can rationally be sanely true to our self,
Accepting our perceptions of disillusionment.

It's amazing how we continue to mistreat,
Others at the expense of selfishness,
Seeking power where none existed,
Dishonoring the very laws of nature.
But there is always lessons to learn,

It's amazing how letters become words,
And can transform, manifest sounds into songs,
Songs of redemption and praise,
Yet many doesn't accept who they are,
Or what to do, so let's be humans first,
A human with an inner soul.

# *When I...*

When i gaze into your eyes
I see God's creation, so beautiful.
Wonderfully, shapen exquisitely made,
Your smile, your melodious laughter,
Fills my very soul, embodying my thoughts.

When i gaze at your face,
See the visions of our ancestors,
Bold, burnt skin, curvy and full.
With sumptuous lips, so inviting,
Spurring my imagination, so tantalizing.

When i see your smile,
I'm reminded of nature in it's true elements,
Fully aglow with myriads of colors.
Like a rainbow with splashes of colors,
So alive, you resonates like a song.

When i see you walking,
You evoke so much passion, so graceful,
I pray i'll be able to keep you close,
Forever in my arms, stabilizing my thoughts,
You'll be my song, my tune,
Playing continuously, forever in my mind.

# *From a slave.....*

From a slave to a president,
A human potential, with intellectual capabilities
Any office of prestige, a mover and a shaper
Of a society so critical of skin color.
Built by people, ancestors of old, sweat, blood and tears.
From a slave to the artist
Who will paint portraits of reality,
Creating realism from brushes of illusion.
Two separate portraits, dangling from the same wall
Bringing to life, the logic of our being.
From a slave to an orator
Spewing words of truth and rights,
Advocation through active representation
Exhibiting the human factors, equalizing the variables
Redemption of the mind, freedom of the spirit.

From a slave, actively in pursuit,
Of that formula of equality, by any means.
Transitioning through time and space,
Regal, royal and proud.

# Dinner for two

Romantic dinner for two,
Dinning by the soft glow of candlelights,
Slow dancing to James Ingram,
Sipping red wine, a mood so right.
Sparkling eyes all aglow,
What's next, who knows.

Romantic dinner for two,
And the vibes is nice,
Jamming to Beres Hammond,
Oh what one dance can do.
Getting all groovy, dancing in the moonlight.
What's next, lady i'm your knight

Romantic dinner for two,
Emotions fever pitched, oh gosh,
Wonder if it's the light or the wine,
Because lady i'M SO INCLINED
Don't need this to end tonight

Romantic dinner for two,
Across the tresh hold i'LL TAKE YOU,
Hanging on to our sexual fantasies
Romance is in the air, passions flying,
Engulfing, consuming the moment,
Romantic dinner for two.

# *Waiting*

She stood waiting in ernest,
As ships arrive and depart,
Leaving behind trails of smoke,
She stamped her feet and wiped her eyes in desperation,
Tears rolling down her cheeks, glistening in the sunshine.
And yet she stood, forbidding herself to go,
She has waited so long time to welcome her love home.

Immaculately dressed, in shimmering colors,
Her face suddenly came alive, like a spring morning.
She caught a glimpse, a shadow of her man,
Tall, fine and stately handsome,
And across the pier, she seems to glide
And down she fell and in desperation up again.
Her waiting has finally come to an end.

She kissed and held him close,
Releasing years of emotions,
A FAITHFUL WOMAN, TRUE TO LOVE,
TEARS OF JOY, HER ONE TRUE LOVE HAS COME HOME.

# I'll stay

I'll stay as long,
As you remain faithful,
To us and what we represent.
I'll stay as long as,
YOU CONTINUE TO BE YOU.
I'LL STAY AS LONG
AS YOU'RE TRUE TO YOURSELF AND GOD,
HARBORING NO FALSEHOOD WHATSOEVER,
I;LL STAY AS LONG AS,
LOVE REMAINS STRONG AND SOLID

I'LL STAY AS LONG
AS YOU CONTINUE TO BE WARM AND TENDER,
TRUE TO THE TIES THAT BINDS US
NEVER WAVERING, AS TRUE AS THE SUNSHINE
AS RIGHT AS THE MOONLIGHT.
I'LL STAY AS LONG AS
YOU COMMIT YOUR ALWAYS
YOUR TIME, YOUR MOMENT, YOUR UNDIVIDED ATTENTION,
TRUE LOVE, MAGNETIZING OUR BEING
KINETIC, .ELECTRIFYING, NEVER LETTING GO
I'LL STAY, SURE I WILL AS THE RAIN.

# We Rise

Like the phoenix we rise above and beyond,
Above alienation, opposition and oppression,
Rising to claim our selfworth, our reality.
Like a beacon in the dark, lighting the pathway,
To meet adversaries, bold and fearless,
SO we rise, we rise beyond and above.
Like the phoenix we rise to proclaim, to acquire,
Our rightful place, restoration of our nationalism,
Standing up for principles which binds us,
CAPTIVATING the indomitable spirit.
a voice for the powerless and the voiceless,
SO WE RISE, WE RISE ABOVE AND BEYOND.
Like the phoenix, we soar to the unknown,
Uncharted boundaries to explore and conquer,
Reclamation of our stolen legacies
iInclination of our past, reachable and attainable
Our dreams and visions realistic.
So we rise, we rise beyond and above.

Like the phoenix we rise from the ashes of self doubts,
To dominate, to realize our true being,
Masters of our destinies, KINGS and QUEENS,
Fathers, mothers, leaders of a free world,
Grasping the the concepts of our origin,
OUR ancestry, our parenthood, and with premium pride we rise,
SO WE RISE, WE RISE ABOVE AND BEYOND.

# *I think about you*

I think about, in so many ways,
You seems to occupy, you always seems to stay,
Deeply embedded in my fragile mind.
Entwined, bonded, giving me,
That loving feeling of belonging.

I think about you,
Even when i know i should not,
Emotions, feelings so strong,
I can't seem to detach myself,
Thinking about you, is as if i'm under a spell,
You leave me in a vibe,
SOME HOW I CAN'T DESCRIBE.

I THINK ABOUT YOU,
YOU'LL FOREVER BE MY HEART BEAT,
YOU MAKE ME SO ALIVE,
I THINK ABOUT YOU,
EVEN WHEN I'M THINKING OF YOU

# *Dreams*

What are dreams made of?
Are dreams made of fallacies,
That overrides our minds,
Causing us to think that,
One day we'l find,
THIS TINY THREAD OF REALITY.
WHATare dreams made of?
Are dreams made of emotions,
Locked up, hidden somewhere,
Buried, trapped in an illusion,
Or is it that dreams,
Are fabrications, never alive or real,
Lost, gone, forgotten forever.
WHAT are dreams made of?
Are dreams machinations of our weakness or our egos,
Which seems to drive many into misconceptions,
So what's really a dream?
IS IT IMAGINATION OR REALISM.

# *Marcus Mosiah Garvey*

Marcus MOSIAH GARVEY, A JAMAICAN AN AFRICAN,
WAS A POOR SON OF SLAVERY,
HE FOUGHT AND WON THE BATTLE FOR DEMOCRACY,
ONE GOD, ONE AIM, ONE DESTINY,
WERE HIS SPOKEN WORDS AND WERE REPEATED ALL OVER.

MARCUS AN ENTREPRENEUR, A POLICTICIAN,
AND ADVOCATE FOR RACE CONSCIOUSNESS,
MARCUS THE PRINTER, THE ORATOR, THE WRITER,
AN IDEALIST, THE WORLD TRAVELLER,
GOING BEYOND FAR AND WIDE, WITH BLACKS AND WHITES
BY HIS SIDE.

MARCUS GARVEY NEVER GAVE UP,
HIS AFRICAN ROOTS OR HIS PRIDE,
EVEN WHEN THE WORLD PUSHED HIM ASIDE
HIS WORK WENT BEYOND HIS HUMAN SCOPE,
HE WAS A PAN AFRICANIST, MARCUS YOUR NAME,
WILL NEVER BE FORGOTTEN, IT'S WITTEN IN OUR Hearts.

# *Precious Mother Earth*

Mother earth is crying, dying
Nuclear construction, destruction, chemical pollution,
Her soil, air and forrest, deforestation
There is no love for her, her dreams and reality no more,
How long will she suffer?
Mother earth is calling out,
Who will lend a listening ear, a hand,
We need to take an environmental stance,
Our streams, gullies and springs,
Are all dumping grounds, contaminated with all sorts of waste.
She is dying slowing, invasion of her royal space.
Mother earth, mother nature is trying yo stay alive,
For our survival our existence,
Her cries cannot go unnoticed, her destruction un seen,
Now toxic algae is riding the tide, global and climatic changes on high,
Mother earth cannot lose her pride,
We have to set our differences aside
She is becoming naked and most afraid,
SHE IS DYING, CRYING OUT FOR OUR HELP.

# Many A Lessons

Many a lessons, as a result of slavery,
Laws, policies to maintain control,
T o feed the power hungry modern plantocracy,
Managers, politicians, chiefs and generals,
Separatists, extremists, wagonists, and antagonists,
All are spokes in the wheel,
The cycle of modern slavery.

Many a lessons, as a result of slavery,
Degrees of alienation, separation, by color and status,
Stratas created to divide and rule and then conquer,
So they continue the distribution of drugs and guns,
To fuel rural and suburban wars,
To eliminate and isolate, all tools of their craft,
Implements of manipulation, tool of race destruction.

Many a lessons as a result of slavery,
Willie LYNCH and JIM CROW LAWS,
Bill of rights and charters, all are faucets,
Instituted, developed to gage our activitism,
To control our thoughts and to curve our movements,
Our very beliefs and culture were threatened,
Even our heritage, so they subdivided,
FIELD SLAVES, FIELD SLAVES AND UNCLE TOMS,
MANY A LESSONS AS A RESULT OF SLAVERY,
BUT WE HAVE COME A LONG WAY, HAVE CROSSED MANY
RIVERS.

# *My Secret Garden*

IN MY SECRET GARDEN,
I FANTASIZE, IMAGINE YOU THERE WITH ME,
HAVING YOU ALL TO MYSELF.
TOUCHING, LAUGHING, SHARING A MOMENT,
EXCHANGING PLEASANTRIES AND EXPLORING EMOTIONS,
EVOKING MOODS, STIMULATING THOUGHTS.

IN MY SECRET GARDEN,
WE STEAL A KISS HERE AND THERE,
ENJOYING EVERY MOMENT IN TIME,
HEARTS POUNDING, TEMPERATURE RISING,
LOVE IS IN THE AIR.

IN MY SECRET GARDEN,
I HOLD YOU CLOSE TO ME,
NOT WANTING TO SUBTRACT NOR DIVIDE,
JUST WANTING TO MAKE EVERY WORDS SPECIAL,
SHARING MY SPACE WITH NO ONE ELSE, THIS IS WHERE I
NEED TO BE.

IN MY SECRET GARDEN,
I HOLD YOUR FACE, I CAN FEEL YOUR BREATH,
SO CLOSE, SO INTIMATE, I LOVE YOUR SMILE,
I'LL TREASURE EACH MOMENT, SO INVALUABLE,
MY SECRET GARDEN, ALL IN MY MIND.

# Tell Me Why

Tell me why the color,
Of my skin, my black skin,
Should be looked upon as a sin,
When i too, was created by GOD,
Tell me why the inner cities,
And their youths are subjected to all sorts of ills
And so we continue to fail the future,
The very prospects, an erosion of self.
Tell me why, we fail to realize,
That slavery and its outcome,
Are suppose to be out platform of change,
Yes the game has changed, taken on a different shape
yet the rules and players are the same
Tell me why do we subject
our selves to be vulnerable, as pawns,
Our civil world has become unbearable, intolerable,
We have to find a way to break this cycle, this monopoly,
SO TELL ME WHY, MY SKIN, MY COLOR,
IS MY BEAUTIFUL SKIN A SIN?

# No Barriers, No Fence

Love has no barriers, nor does it runs a wire fence,
Love is never for sale nor rental,
Loves not a candy on a shelf,
Love will conquer all, even our fears

Through good or bad times,
love is all forgiving
Love is pure of heart, there is no greater joy,
Love is the that musical beat, the chord,
SO harmonious, so fulfilling, warm and sincere.

LOVE is like a magnetic field,
IT pulls and attracts, love binds and cements,
LOVE has no radius or circumference,
Love has no angles or degrees,
NO longitude or latitude, no class, color or creed,
We were created in love, by love.

LOVE is the only common thread,
Extending globally, breaking all records,
Smashing down all walls of insincerity,
Connecting people through the medium of truth,
Love is the ultimate.

# No Pleasure

I find no pleasure in your system,
For hundreds of years, you have manipulated,
Served on your platter, lies and deceit.
Masked your words and actions so meticulous

From plato to socrates,
The mother land africa,
To the roman empire,
Nothing has changed, the stories and scripts are the same,
Only the names and characters have changed.

Find no pleasure in your system,
Which has made us all victims,
OF circumstances, draining our sustenance.
Our heritage and history were stolen,
And were given diluted falsehood,
Books of ideology, unreflective of our ancestry.

I find no pleasure in your system,
Which hunted and chained us as animals,
A system that continues to divide us
Erecting your modern day corporate plantations,
A SYSTEM that tries to chain our thoughts,
But redemption is a must,
Its only in god, in him we rest our trust

# Just A Smile

Oh what one smile can do,
A simple, single smile,
One so warm, strong and attractive.
A Smile to always remember,
One to spend an entire life time with

A SMILE says a million words,
So effortless and suggestive,
One so deep, and fathomless.
Smile and feel good about yourself,
Your smile is a reflection of ones self.

Oh smile, let there be no regrets,
Smile because you really mean it,
Please smile and illuminate the place,
Allow your beautiful smile to set the pace,
Smile and show your grace.

Oh what a smile can do,
Smile and let the world smile too,
Truly the world will smile back at you,
So don't hold back, release yourself,
Laugh, smile don't hold it in.
Smile and release your reality.

# Unchained

Absentee fathers, frustrated mothers,
So the children feed s on seeds,
Of anger and utter resentment.
Hatred, breeds shottas, gangsters,
It's a like a concrete jungle out here.

Broken children, marginalized childhood,
Pathetic parenting misguided individuals,
Chained opportunities, strained relationships,
So there are souls on fire, blazing anger.,
And so the cycle continues.
SILENCE, indifference of opinions,
MANY INNOCENTS becoming the victims,

Diluted hope, broken promises,
Miseducated children, chained capabilities,
SO OUR FUTURE IS LOOKING ALMOST DIM,
RISE UP CHILDREN, GO AND CLAIM YOUR TRIUMP,
UNLOCK THE CHAINS, WHICH HAVE HELD YOU SO LONG.

# Echoes of Time

Until the idea of eye or skin,
Color, creed is far gone, forgotten,
There shall no peace among mankind,
No matter the moment in time.
There will be power struggle, to no end,

From the town ship to the ghettos,
The cries are the the same,
There will always be changes, as time echoes in.
Echoes of victimization and brutality,
Riots and bloodshed, polictical and religious changes,
PEOPLE all confused frustrated of the system.

So the old mill continues to turn,
Giving rise to the cycle of violence,
Domestic violence, broken home, broken marriages,
Gone are the days of fun,
THOSE DAYS ARE REPLACED BY GUNS,
SO THE ECHOES ARE HEARD BEYOND.

Yes its the same story, of history and selfless glory,
From the plantations to the suburbs,
ECHOES of time, echoes of time.,
Blowing all of our minds,
Its a race for truth, fallacy versus ideology.

# Mama

Mama has been through a lot,
She has been battered and bruised,
Oh yes, seduced, and abused.
Mistreated by a prefect lie,
Totally an affair of the heart,
Domestic violence is so unkind.

Mama gloried the very ground he walked,
She bore his children too,
Mama cooked, washed and kept,
The habitat spotlessly clean,
Yet mama was always treated so mean
Domestic violence is so unkind.

Mama has been so broken, at the verge,
Of irrationality, her self image,
Taken and her confidence shaken at its roots,
Mama friends have noticed her change
But no one under stood her pain.
Drugs, alcohol have now became her sole companion,
DOMESTIC VIOLENCE IS SO UNKIND.

# *Our Children*

Where will our children play?
When these roads, streets are not safe anymore.
Legal murderers, hired guns in clubs and stores,
Our playgrounds are battle grounds,
Killzone, war zones for gangsters and police

Where will our children grow,
When race profiling drives fear like a stench,
Bus stops, classrooms even the park,
Our next generation prospects seems dark,
Our children are endangered species,
And our heritage at risk.
WHERE will our children feel free,
To eat, play, to be socially stimulated,
When it seems no where is safe anymore,
Home invasion, spikes in police brutality,
At risk youths, unemployment, poverty, it;s a mental torture.
Where will our children pray,
When our places of worship are being bombed and burnt,
Total injustice of race and religion,
Disregard of civil liberties, religious freedom in violation
OUR VERY EXISTENCE AT RISK,
SO TELL ME, WHERE WILL OUR CHILDREN,
PLAY, GROW, FEEL FREE, HAVE FUN.

# I Was Born

I was born with my black skin,
From a black womb, into this world,
So don't tell me, i was born,
In sin or shapened in iniquity.
I'm a human with my individual identity,
Proud of who i am.

I was born with my melanin,
Bronze, burnt royally made.
Roots from the African shores.
A voice, a human, respecting all,
Whether chinese, indian, whatever creed,
Proud to be me, born to be free.

Was born with all my faculties,
All intact, with knowledge and imaginations,
Though misunderstood, mistreated,
Shelved as colonial tools, chattels for sale.
Controlled, alienated and brainwashed,
We are only owned by creation,
Irrespective of our circumstances.

I was born with this burnt african skin,
Proud to be me, this is who i am,
Ready to make strides in a world seen through lenses,
Colored by inferiority and classism,
My color is my reality, my voice, my circumstances.

# I'll Never

My love, i'll never find,
The words to say my love,
Words aren't enough to show my appreciation,
I will have to exhibit tis in a different way,
No amount of actions or mere words.

We have evolved as one, truly can't explain
My love, I'll never find the words,
The song, the tune to sing,
Nor the chords, the lines to write, to describe,
No amount of time will suffice,
Our connections, so heavenly so celestial.

My love i'll never find the words,
To justify my inclinations,
Mere passions, emotions can't express,
Your love is so refreshing, as soothing as the rain,
Drumming on my window pane.

My love, I'll never find
You'll never find, a love like ours,
No need to search no more,
Our love will take on wings, forever we'll soar

# WE play, we cry

We play, we cry,
We all feel the hurt,
Imposed on us by our different circumstances,
Sometimes beyond our human control,
Locked in our consciousness, keeping us subjected,
So we cling to ideas, concepts and perceptions,
Some unrealistic to our being.

We play, we cry together,
We all feel the pain, caused by our actions,
Yet we all can feel the rain drops,
As we accept the manifestations of self proclamation,
Geared towards having us docile and in servitude.

We play, we cry collectively,
And then we ask the question,
Sometimes surprised at the answers,
Some beyond our scope of comprehension
Caught in the middle stuck in oblivion,
Trying to rationalize, to equate reality versus practicality.

So we play, we cry, we try,
To withstand the whims and fantasy,
Sometimes forgetting we're humans,
Prone to errors, readily misunderstood,
Accepting the circumstances we can't change,
SO WE PLAY, WE CRY, WE CLING TO OUR SANITY.

# *Jamaica Pon Mi Mind*

I can still hear the christmas rooster crowing fearfully,
In the back yard coop,
Saying thanks, it's not yet christmas.
As echoes of the early farmers, getting ready for the early toil,
Early birds singing, butterflies flaunting, bees buzzing.
From the house, the sensation of fried dumplings,
And the aroma of the chocolate tea.
Jamaica pon mi mind.

I still can hear the crickets and see the peenie wallie,
Flying in their space like fighter jets,
And the smell of the wood fire,
I still can smell the kerosene oil,
And the glow from the Home SWEET HOME LAMP,
The melodic drip of water in the metal bath pan,
Jamaica won mi mind.

I remember when we use to bundle up,
And would listen to duppy stories, boy we were so afraid,
That night no one would enter their room,
So the living room was the camp for the night.
Cornmeal pudding wid coffee tea,
Blue draws and drops.
Jamaica won mi mind.

Christmas time was my favorite time of the year,
CAROL SINGING IN THE EARLY MAWNING,
BRAKING MASS TOM CANE AND STEALING MAS JOE NAVEL
ORANGES.
Playing dandy shandy and the merry ring games,

Eating the good ole rum cake with the strong sorrel drinks,
And on christmas day, the curried goat, stew pork and stewed rooster,
AND of course redstripe beers and de good ole white rum.
JAMAICA PON MI MIND.

# Sweet Millie Mango

I took a bite, a deep bite,
And i savored the taste,
Umm, so sweet and juicy,
I could not contain the juices,
I had no choice but to let it run down my cheeks

I paused, and carefully took,
Another bite, attacking it from the other side
This bite tasted even better,
So i bit in more, passionately,
Didn't want to miss the sweetness.

The pleasure, the joy so over whelming,
This was my very first time,
So i took bites after bites, so delicious,
I caressed what was left,
I was almost near my climax.

Finally i was finished and i felt so good,
My only annoyance was the hairs,
That were dangling from my teeth
My first time, sweet mango,
millie mango so sweet.

# Oh Mother

Must have cried a million tears,
As i saw her being lowered,
Lying in her casket, surrounded by wreaths of flowers,
I knew then, my sorrowful journey has just began,
And i know i got to be strong.
MOTHER lived a full life,
She gave us her all for many years,
Mother planted the seeds of morality,
So our transition into adulthood would be smooth,
She always told us, 'education is the key'
And as i watched her making the transition
Into this dark hole, I will never forget her role
Mother was a mentor, i remembered clearly,
She'stood tall at all time, unwavering
I know for sure, i'll surely miss,
Her bedtime stories and her late night kiss.
Oh mother, you were my rock,
Journey on mother, you have ran you race
Forever we'll be grateful, no word can't expressed
Sleep on mother, go and take your rest.

# Transplanted

Transplanted were our ancestors
Millions of black bodies, across the ATLANTIC,
From AFRICA to the West Indies, to the AMERICAS
Goods, merchandises, wares for sale,
Men, women and children all units of labor.

Uprooted were our fore parents,
Kings, queens, princes and princesses.
To the unknown, chained and shackled,
Lost souls, in the belly of these beastly ships
Stacked, packed, destined for commerce

Historically came the Portuguese,
Then the dutch, the spanish and the english too,
All were allies and competitors for this valuable cargo,.
Not to be forgotten were our very own africans,
They were active participants, bestowing pain and misery on their own

These very transplanted, transported, uprooted souls,
Have helped to to carve, and have created today's culture, music and politics,
World views and diversity differences,
There was no substitute, their contributions were absolute
Inventors, innovators, contributors to modern esthetics.

# Bridges, Walls and Fences

We build walls so high and towering,
Surrounding us to be unreachable.
We make fences and build bridges,
Creating blockades of defenses,
To keep out, to hide,
Our selves, our feelings.

We trod various pathways,
Some smooth, some rugged,
To reach the unthinkable,
Summit of our near prefect life,
Running the race to win,
Shaping our future from the past.

We detach our selves,
From the clutches of circumstances,
Dismantling the chains, the barriers,
The Walls of mistrust and hatred
Then comes the acceptance of the truth,
Grossing the parallels of time

Ultimately we build bridges, m end fences
To reconnect, repair that which was broken
So we renew our hopes and aspirations
For the freedom of the spirit,
We build, bridges, walls and erect, repair fences.

# *Marcus Garvey teachings*

Give us the teachings of marcus mosiah garvey,
Jamaica's champion for rights and equality,
Leader and founder of the UNIA,
They saw him as a threat,
Just because of his ideals and deeds,
So give us the teachings of marcus mosiah garvey.

Give us the teachings of marcus garvey,
Let them resonate, filling the reservoirs of our minds,
Evoking, awaking a generation,
Recognition of our power within,
MARCUS planted this seed, seeds of race redemption,
An acceptance of influence, through MARTIN LUTHER AND
MALCOLM X.
So give us the teachings of marcus mosiah garvey

Give us the teachings of marcus mosiah,
Come let them be our guide, our testimony,
One god, one aim, one destiny,
Garvey said, 'UP YE MIGHTY RACE ',
He saw the world not through a color scheme,
Marcus the scholar, the orator, the educator,
So give us the teachings of marcus mosiah garvey.

# *Just Me*

Just have to be me
,Black resilient and practical,
AS REAL, NOT AFAKE,
Nor a figment of someone's imagination,
The lion, the king, the golden child.

I just have to be me,
Calm, forthright not inflated,
STRAIGHT FROM THE AFRICAN WOODSTOCK
MY PARENT'S LAST SON, ALL ME.

I have to be me,
From a family where love,
WAS always important and was provided.
A PRAGMATIST, A REALIST A VOICE
VOCAL AND PURPOSEFUL, TRUE TO THE BONE.

I HAVE TO BE ME,
TRUE TO MY FAULTS AND FRAILITIES,
ACCEPTING WHO I AM, PROUD AND STRONG
BEING ME, I HAVE TO BE ME.

# Remnants of Slavery

Remnants and echoes of slavery,
Still vivid in my mind.
Bonded, binded and chained.
Packed, stacked, all goods for sale,
Taken forcibly from our homeland, into lands unknown.

Echoes and remnants of slavery,
Promoted, enabled by our very own flesh and blood,
Some for fame, others for fortune,
Changing our lifestyles, erasing our royal names.
And yes we have arrived, and have acknowledged,
Our trek across the ATLANTIC, was about the race war.
Echoes and remnants of slavery,
Arabs, Dutch, English and French,
Christians, quakers and presidents too.
We were all merchandises for sale,
Millions of naked bodies, women, men and helpless children.
Echoes and remnants of slavery,
human flesh for sale on the open market,
Echoes of voices of the anguished,
Voices of the sufferings.

# Guns, Thugs and The Garrison

From the garrisons to the slums,
Young bloods graduating from guns and knives,
Roaming the streets, to the avenues,
Down the ghettos, through the lanes,
Mothers weep, sisters and brothers feel the pain.

From the skates to carts,
To the crude market stalls,
Retaliation is the only known code,
Guns barking, machines blazing,
Camouflage zinc fences, everybody running in fear
Sadly, no one seems to care.

Another victim by gun violence,
A possible potential dies in silence in the street,
Smashed and crushed dreams,
All victims of a vicious scheme,
Politicians, drug lords and area dons,
Cries goes unanswered, from the gaza to the gully banks, the turf and the
block.

Children watchfully and fearfully play,
Even the very animals are afraid to stray,
Guns crews, thugs and hoodlums,
The garrison is their reality, the guns their songs.

# Boss Man

Good morning boss, yeah you boss!
From last month i;ve been wanting to talk to you,
Would love to address your general attitude,
Please, no disrespect meant, but we all are on the fence,
Boss don't look at me that way, don't walk away,
Not trying to be insubordinate, nor implying insolence.

Boss we all rights to freedom of expression
Without disrespecting your status or your office,
I can see you're still in shock,
But you see boss man we all got your back,
So let manners balance the work space,
From pants to skirts to frock.
Slow down and simmer boss man,
Let's all sit and reason,
Come boss set the pace, let's converse,
Boss man you affi set the trend,
And trust mi mi nuh mean to offend
It's just my working respect i man a defend.

# Life's Value

Do we value the life of another,
Or do we just fool our selves
Pretending to be our brothers and sisters keeper
So we inflate, to dominate others existence,
Trying to justify our beliefs.

So with scant regards or remorse
We under value the role of others,
Even parents, forgetting the super role played by our ancestors.
They all have toiled and have paved tis very way,
So that you and i can attain, without alienation or intimidation.

So up ye mighty race,
Go out and accomplish whatever ones heart desires,
Place some value on others and our selves,
Let's strive to rid this society of wanton thinking of immorality,
Price and value are variants, let's equalize the variables.
Come let's value life.

,

## Play Me Some Music

Play me some music, mister DJ,
Play me some JOHNHOLT
Spin me some GARNET SIIK,
Mix me some conscious music
MINE ears are sick from hearing the slackness.

Play me some Dennis Brown,
So i can generate some loving feelings.
Put on the turn table, some Gregory Issac,
SO I can get me a night nurse
Yes i'll be most gracious mister DJ.

Play me some Beres Hammond,
To soothe and revitalize,
Just to bring back the vibes.
Fling on Mr. ALTON ELLIS,
So i can sit and chill
Getting ready for a dancing mood.

Play me some music,
Mista DJ, play me, play it for me,
Nice and easy, haul and pull up,
So play me some music,
I TRULY WONT REFUSE IT.

# \Today, Tomorrow

If tomorrow comes not,
Rejoice with the promise of today.
Live and fulfill all your wishes,
Today is a reality, tomorrow a mere fantasy,
Maybe a thought, an imagination.

Today is the the day we toil,
Exerting our shoulders to the wheel.
Assisting the weak, the depressed.
Those trodded on with not a glimpse of compromise,
Tomorrow is a wish, a sullen promise, today is reality.

Today is our time to live,
To give account of our action,
Tomorrow i may never live to give
Possibly to myself or others,
Today should be our reality, tomorrow only GOD knows.

# *Redemption*

Redemption! Oh what a powerful sound,
Heard from the lips of every humans.
Irrespective of color, race or creed,
But do we know the meaning?,
IT's the liberation of self, people, mind and ultimately the heart.
Redemption, is being ready, to stamp out,
To crush oppression, to make the stance against,
All forms of injustice, in any form or shape.

Redemption is totally universal,
Without guile, prejudice or favor,
It knows no language or barriers,
Redemption is our rights to choose life,
Even if our choice comes at a cost,
Truly redemption should never be lost.

# *The Rain*

I sat listening to the rain,
And it sang lovely tune,
So clear and melodious,
Pit, pat, pitta, patta, pit.

As i sat listening,
The rain seems to drive,
My mental and physical pain away.
Speaking to me softly and silently,
Making me feel so happy and free.

The rain left a fresh scent so heavenly,
In it's aftermath, fragrances of all sorts,
Roses, jasmines, magigolds and lavenders,
Natural water filling the earth's reservoir, calming the soil.

Plants, flowers, birds and bees,
All greet the rain with their happy songs,
Replenishing the gullies, the river and the streams,
Running it's marathon finally to the sea.
And oh how i love the rain,
As it raps against my frosted window pane.

# Haita

The degradation and squalor amazed me,
As I sat in wonderment and horror.
Can a place so potentially rich,
Be lost in economic and political gloom.
I could smell the stench blowing in the breeze,
Poverty has claimed another nation.

Ragged, desperate and frightened people,
Despondent and scampering by, searching amongst the rubble for scraps,.
To see such inhumane conditions, bought tears to my eyes.
Actions of politics, greed and social murderers,
Sadly have made their presence felt.

These people, the fist independent nation,
Have been given the keys to false hope and prosperity.
ALIENATED, NEGLECTED ALMOST FORGOTTEN.

# Imagine

Imagine if there was no world,
And there were no wars nor peace,
Would humanity be the same,
Imagine there were no words,
No songs, no instruments to play.
Would we still co exist.?

Imagine riding on the wings of change,
Breaking down barriers, rearranging our situations,
Searching for an elusive resolve with absolution.
Changing self and world views, so timeless.
Imagine if there was no world
.

Imagine there was no sun,
nor wind, or rain, no summer nor spring.
THERE were no bees or bird to sing.
ALL common threads of rationale gone,
Imagine a world without oxygen.

So we're merely clinging, surviving by instincts,
So like preys and predators we survive.
We cast all fears and doubts, mere contributors.
No more love, so we hate, we kill and abuse.
Imagine if there was no world.

Imagine if time stood still, became timeless,


And peace a glimpse, a fraction of itself,
Just scenes from a movie, all staged and televised,
A place where the innocents are chastised and ostracized.
Imagine, just imagine if there was no world.

# *They Say*

They say we are free,
And yet we are not equal.
Through the passage of time,
Situation has dictated how a race, a culture,
Must be controlled, restrained.

They say we are free,
And yet we are burdened by,
A misguided system geared,
Towards segregation and race hatred,
So the years go by, and we continues to be maligned

They say we are free,
Free to express, to speak and to seek,
That one true meaning, fulfillment,
Our reality of being human, respected, not alienated.

They say we are free,
And yet our streets aren't safe anymore,
People are afraid to roam,
To play to worship or to call a place a home,
Unfortunately still tied to these chains,
Yet they say we are free.

# The Struggle Continues

The struggle continues,
As time passes, colored and blanketed,
Everyday we are reminded of the pain,
Cruelly endured by those before us.
Beatened chained, treated so inhumane,
Utterly belittled a people with no voice.
Yet the struggle continues.

The struggle continues,
So we are reminded of our ancestry,
Reflecting on the mother land of the Blue Nile,
Innocent people, stacked and shackled in a single file,
Unfortunate chattels for sale, goods for the auction.
Yet the struggle continues.

The struggle continues,
And we have made immense strides,
Standing proud, royal and presidential,
Unwavering in or stance, to be free,
Safe guarding the future for to.
Yet the struggle continues

The struggle continues,
As we try to safe guard our legacy,
So this institution won't be forgotten,
Knowing the race is not yet won,
Many river to cross and songs to sing.
Yet the struggle continues.

# Rivers to Cross

Many rivers to cross,
Yes the journey has began,
Some fences, obstacles, and barriers,
Our will to survive, to conquer.
Many fears, numerous triumphs

Many rivers to cross,
Some will never know how,
Opportunities wasted, bonds broken,
Battles won, victors, accepting defeat,
Limits on survival, seeking revival.

Many rivers to cross,
Let's build a bridge.
So we can lessen the journey, be connected,
Renewed in confidence, awakening our perspective,
A people with a spirit,
With our own individuality.

Many river to cross,
So we have to navigate carefully,
Around, over and across,
Never going under, collectively surviving,
Our strength lies in our unity, together we'll find a way.
Many rivers to cross.

# Seasons CHANGE

As the season changes,
And autumn becomes winter,
Spring bumps into summer,
So is the journey of humanity,
Always evolving into something new.

As the season changes,
So does our innate abilities and personalities,
Our concepts and characteristics, our commonalities,
Always searching for this perfect union,
A bond to connect to shape to exist.

As the season changes,
So too is our ideals and wishes,
We aspire to be the best, but not at other expense.
For some this is a mere competition, a food chain
But the truth is not superficial, it runs deep.

As the season changes,
We are reminded of the ancient journey,
Yet we all are on the same pathway,
With varying wants and needs,
Seeking redemption, accepting changes.

As the season changes,
Sometimes our circumstances collide, merges
Wild, untamed and very diverse,
So as a people we summon all our resilience to overcome,
All possible obstacles, all barriers, as the season change.

# Festive Rebirth

Christmas, a time of festive rebirth,
We give, we dine enjoying planet earth,
Spending precious moments with friends and families,
Decked christmas trees, all a colorful sight,
Illuminated by the lovely moonlight

Christmas, a time of words and moods,
As we meet and greet families,
Laughing and singing around the festive tables,
Drinking and eating, eggnog, juices and wines,
FOODS on exhibitions, for this special time.

Christmas, a time of the arctic snow,
Whether winter or the tropical sunshine,
Wherever we live or reside,
The mood and vibe is the same,
Christmas is a time to celebrate,


Even though for some it's not the same
Some wandering cold and hungry, without a name.
And as we gather to feast, remember those,
Not so fortunate to eat or drink,
Hue of colors on display, just to name a few,
Sunday morning bells are sounding,
Christmas messages from the pastor's pew,
Christmas, a time of festive rebirth.

# *Glamorised*

Glamorized policies and laws
Have caused little-bo-peep,
To lose his only sheep,
His eyes could not believe, he saw the dish running with his spoon.
And you can imagine, the little dog laughing,
After he lost his only bone.

Glamorized politicians and the people,
And the people continues to suffer, though hopeful.
Another JACK AND THE BEAN STALK,
Alice is trapped in wonder land,
Unsatisfied gratifications leads to misguided judgements,
So the ends don't justify the means.

Glamorized leaders, all power hungry,
Selfish and unsympathetic to the people's call,
Truly pride cometh before a fall,
History has taught us so many lessons,
From CONSTANTINE, to STALIN, to Adolf Hitler.

Glamorized weapons created for man's destruction,
Have created waves of pain and trauma,
BIO chemical weapons to promote the order,
Laws, clauses and policies to gender control,
Resolute we stand, not straying away from the foal.

# Musical Evolution

Jamaica's music has evolved,
From mento, ska to rocksteady,
To heavy new beats of reggae.
An evolution of bouncing dumping, limitless rhythms,
All have made reggae music unique.
Reggae gave birth to rap and pop genre
WE HAVE SEEN RAPPERS AND SOUL BROTHERS TOO.

Listen the congo beat, this pounding drum,
Beats, rhythms and blues, all jazzy in feelings,
Sounds and words blending in harmony,
So sweet to the ears, appealing to the soul.
From maestro, to legends and kings,
Reggae has conquered the air wave.

Reggae is our voice, our symbol,
A lifestyle, a movement
From a evolution to a revolution,
Connecting people from all continents,
Cultures, class, creed and skin.
Whether one drop, soca, disco or pop.
This is one evolution they cannot stop.

From vinyl, to cassettes, to discs to drives,
Our music has evolve,
From the corners to the lanes,
Cherry Gardens to downtown, newyork to hollywood,
Reggae has captured ears an audiences for all over,
Our music tells our stories, our journey.

# *Codes of Color*

Torn from culture and families
Imported and exported to colonies afar,
Cold grounds and rock stones,
HAVE SOMETIMES BEEN OUR BEDS,
Let's salute LINDA BROWN and celebrate ROSA PARKS
Yes states laws were black codes,
MEASURES OF CONTROL, RESTRICTING MOBILITY.
CODES OF COLOR.

Voting rights were instituted,
Solely controlled by policies, all vehicles of segregation,
People of color were not allowed to enter from the front,
Whether on a bus or a building, restrictions in public spaces,
Maids and janitors, bell hops or butlers,
codes of color.

SEPARATED communities segregated churches,
Separations in elementary, middle and high schools,
WORLDWIDE THE AFFECTS AND EFFECTS ARE FELT,
But our stories must be heard, must be told,
WE ARE RESPONSIBLE FOR OUR STORY
Will never allow others to tell our history.
codes of color.

# *Passage of Time*

Ethnocentrism, the inclusion, exclusion of the black race.
Alienated through ethnicity, arrested by our skin tone.
Our views, ideologies permanently crushed by circumstances,
Misunderstood, faded in the background of time.
Yet we bleed the same color blood, and brains the same weight.

Race prejudice, discrimination have compelled,
A race to identify its roots, our africaness
Whilst overlooking the stereotypical, feeling inferior,
Africans were called savages and heathens,
Uncivilized beings, with the need to be colonized, chastised, christianized.

Dehumanized, to the extent of mental depravity,
The family, the community were the only sanity,
From territory to territory, from plantation to plantation,
Pitiless, ruthless masters, uncaring, unforgiving mistresses.
Those who were recalcitrant wore stripes of cruelty.

All through these struggles blacks reestablished,
And recreated movements of upliftments,
Began black businesses, schools, churches and were even active in
government,
The black power movement became not only a thrust,
But also a pathway to african and world consciousness.
A vehicle, a gate way to self actualization.

Black unity, black power became the embodiment,
Of Pan Africanism, a celebration of truth,
Basically a medium of racial disparity, crushed, destroyed,
Yet not forgotten, fractionally etched in our minds,
A duplication of our experience, a replication of our past, a glimpse of the
future.

# Give Thanks

Give thanks for life,
For each day we rise and see the sun
Don't you ever let a moment slip,
Whether chilling or having fun,.
Life is our greatest gift,
So let's give thanks for life.

Give thanks for life,
Even when the road gets rocky,
And the hills and valleys get steep.
Just utter a prayer and hold a sleep,
Life is a never ending journey.
So give thanks for life.

Give thanks for life,
Life didn't promise a bed of roses,
There will be times of sunshine and times of rainfall,
Never take for granted the lessons of life,
Life is like a bicycle, remember to pedal and balance.
So give thanks for life.

Give thanks for life,
No matter the choices or circumstances,
Never get frustrated or broken,
Many a words are best left unspoken.
Life is an invaluable asset, worth more than precious metals.
So let's give thanks for life.

# They See Me Smile

ONLY GOD KNOWS, ONLY GOD KNOWS,
They see me smile,
And i may laugh like a child.
Yet you don't know what i feel inside,
Or what i endure daily,
You don't know my fears, my triumphs or aspirations.

They see me smile,
And i may flaunt about like a butterfly,
But you'll never see me cry,
Even when i'm broken inside,
However laden or burdened by circumstances.

They see me smile,
And yet deep inside i'm dying
Nevertheless i'll keep on trying,
The human spirit is a reservoir of strength,
No matter the rhyme or the reason,
Brother man the time or the season.

They see me smile,
Pretense has been my best friend,
So i learn to build these walls so high
So as not to expose my true feelings, my emptiness.
I hid myself, concealed my fears and anxieties.
They see me smile, but they don't know what i feel inside.

# I Fell in Love

I fell in love with her,
From the tender age of eleven,
The same year my grandmother,
Made her celestial transition to heaven.
She became my very best friend and companion,
And i was so in love

She would have me up late at nights,
Just scribbling on my note pad,
All sorts of love verses, my little room emotionally charged,
Stimulating every cell, every single neuron in my fragile body,
These moments so magical, a journey into wonderland.
And i was so in love.

We would converse in silent tones,
Pens, pencils, note books and the mind.
Sometimes drifting, losing track of time,
Exhausting as it was, these were my treasured moments,
She was never a bore, even at times i would get sore.
And i was so in love.

And as the years progressed
Our relationship became golden,
There was no other like you around.
You made me me the laughing stock at school,
And in class, i would fall asleep, which wasn't cool,
And i was so in love.

You drew my attention to detail,
From alphabets, words, syllabications and sentence formations,

I was duly taught to horne my craft,
ESTATIC WHEN I PASSED MY FIRST DRAFT
I FELL IN LOVE, AND STILL IS IN LOVE,
WITH THE ART OF POETRY, SO PURE.

Printed in the United States
By Bookmasters

Printed in the United States
By Bookmasters